The Story of

Billy the Kid

As told by

Charles A. Siringo

in 1920

Illustrations by
Badgley Publishing Company

2012

ISBN: 978-0-9854403-3-6

This book is part of the Historical Collection of Badgley Publishing Company and has been transcribed from the original. The original contents have been edited and corrections have been made to original printing, spelling and grammatical errors when not in conflict with the author's intent to portray a particular event or interaction. Annotations have been made and additional contents may have been added by Badgley Publishing Company in order to clarify certain historical events or interactions and to enhance the author's content. Fonts have been changed from the original printing to make the book easier to read. Photos and illustrations from the original may have been touched up, enhanced and sometimes enlarged for better viewing. Additional illustrations and photos have been added by Badgley Publishing Company.

Lincoln, New Mexico

INTRODUCTION

The author feels that he is capable of writing a true and unvarnished history of "Billy the Kid," as he was personally acquainted with him, and assisted in his capture, by furnishing Sheriff Pat Garrett with three of his fighting cowboys—Jas. H. East, Lee Hall and Lon Chambers.

The facts set down in this narrative were gotten from the lips of "Billy the Kid," himself, and from such men as Pat Garrett, John W. Poe, Kip McKinnie, Charlie Wall, the Coe brothers, Tom O'Folliard, Henry Brown, John Middleton, Martin Chavez, and Ash Upson. All these men took an active part, for or against, the "Kid." Ash Upson had known him from childhood, and was considered one of the family, for several years, in his mother's home.

Other facts were gained from the lips of Mrs. Charlie Bowdre, who kept "Billy the Kid" hid out at her home in Fort Sumner, New Mexico, after he had killed his two guards and escaped.

CHAS. A. SIRINGO.

Lincoln County Courthouse

CHAPTER I.

BILLY BONNEY KILLS HIS FIRST TWO MEN, AND BECOMES
A DARING OUTLAW IN THE REPUBLIC OF MEXICO.

In the slum district of the great city of New York, on the 23rd day of November, 1859, a blue-eyed baby boy was born to William H. Bonney and his good looking, auburn haired young wife, Kathleen. Being their first child he was naturally the joy of their hearts. Later, another baby boy followed.

In 1862 William H. Bonney shook the dust of New York City from his shoes and emigrated to Coffeeville, Kansas, on the northern border of the Indian Territory, with his little family.

Soon after settling down in Coffeeville, Mr. Bonney died. Then the young widow moved to the Territory of Colorado, where she married a Mr. Antrim.

Shortly after this marriage, the little "family of four" moved to Santa Fe, New Mexico, at the end of the old Santa Fe trail.

Here they opened a restaurant, and one of their first boarders was Ash Upson, then doing work on the Daily New Mexican.

Little, blue-eyed Billy Bonney, was then about five years of age and became greatly attached to good natured, jovial, Ash Upson, who spent much of his leisure time playing with the bright boy.

Three years later, when the hero of our story was about eight years old, Ash Upson and the Antrim family pulled up stakes and moved to the booming silver mining camp of Silver City, in the southwestern part of the Territory of New Mexico.

Ash Upson

Here Mr. and Mrs. Antrim established a new restaurant, and had Ash Upson as the star boarder.

Naturally their boarders were made up of all classes, both women and men, —some being gamblers and toughs of the lowest order.

Amidst these surroundings, Billy Bonney grew up. He went to school and was a bright scholar. When not at school, Billy was associating with tough men and boys, and learning the art of gambling and shooting.

This didn't suit Mr. Antrim, who became a cruel step-father, according to Billy Bonney's way of thinking.

Jesse Evans, a little older than Billy, was a young tough who was a hero in Billy's estimation. They became fast friends, and bosom companions. In the years to come they were to fight bloody battles side by side, as friends, and again as bitter enemies.

As a boy, Mr. Upson says Billy had a sunny disposition, but when aroused had an uncontrollable temper.

At the tender age of twelve, young Bonney made a trip to Fort Union, New Mexico, and there gambled with the negro soldiers. One "black nigger' cheated Billy, who shot him dead. This story I got from the lips of "Billy the Kid" in 1878.

Making his way back to Silver City he kept the secret from his fond mother, who was the idol of his heart.

One day Billy's mother was passing a crowd of toughs on the street. One of them made an insulting remark about her. Billy, who was in the crowd, heard it. He struck the fellow in the face with his fist and then picked up a rock from the street. The "tough" made a rush at Billy, and as he passed Ed. Moulton he planted a blow back of his ear, and laid him sprawling on the ground.

This act cemented a friendship between Ed. Moulton and the future young outlaw.

About three weeks later Ed Moulton got into a fight with two toughs in Joe Dyer's saloon. He was getting the best of the fight. The young blacksmith who had insulted Mrs. Antrim and who had been knocked down by Ed. Moulton, saw a chance for revenge. He rushed at Moulton with an uplifted chair. Billy Bonney was standing nearby, on nettles, ready to render assistance to his benefactor, at a moment's notice. The time had now arrived. He sprang at the blacksmith and stabbed him with a knife three times. He fell over dead.

Billy ran out of the saloon, his right hand dripping with human blood.

Now to his dear mother's arms, where he showered her pale cheeks with kisses for the last time.

Realizing the result of his crime, he was soon lost in the pitchy darkness of the night, headed towards the southwest, afoot. For three days and nights Billy wandered through the cactus covered hills, without seeing a human being.

Luck finally brought him to a sheep camp, where the Mexican herder gave him food.

From the sheep camp he went to McKnight's ranch and stole a horse, riding away without a saddle.

Three weeks later a boy and a grown man rode into Camp Bowie, a government post. Both were on a skinny, sore-back pony. This new found companion had a name and history of his own, which he was nursing in secret. He gave his name to Billy as "Alias," and that was the name he was known by around Camp Bowie.

Finally Billy, having disposed of his sore-back pony, started out for the Apache Indian Reservation, with "Alias," afoot. They were armed with an old army rifle and a six-shooter, which they had borrowed from soldiers.

About ten miles southwest of Camp Bowie these two young desperados came onto three Indians, who had twelve ponies, a lot of pelts and several saddles, besides good fire-arms, and blankets. In telling of the affair afterwards, Billy said: "It was a ground-hog case. Here were twelve good ponies, a supply of blankets, and five heavy loads of pelts. Here were three blood-thirsty savages reveling in luxury and refusing help to two free-born, white, American citizens, foot-sore and hungry. The plunder had to change hands. As one live Indian could place a hundred United States soldiers on our trail, the decision was made.

"In about three minutes there were three dead Indians stretched out on the ground, and with their ponies and plunder we skipped. There was no fight. It was the softest thing I ever struck."

About one hundred miles from this bloody field of battle, the surplus ponies and plunder were sold and traded off to a band of Texas emigrants.

Finally the two young brigands settled down in Tucson, where Billy's skill as a Monte dealer, and card player kept them in luxuriant style, and gave them prestige among the sporting fraternity.

Becoming tired of town life, the two desperadoes hit the trail for San Simon, where they beat a band of Indians out of a lot of money in a "fake" horse race.

The next we hear of Billy Bonney is in the State of Sonora, Old Mexico, where he went alone, according to his own statement.

In Sonora he joined issues with a Mexican gambler named Melquiades Segura. One night the two murdered a Monte dealer, Don Jose Martinez, and secured his "bank roll."

Now the two desperadoes shook the dust of Sonora from their feet and landed in the city of Chihuahua, the capital of the State of Chihuahua, several hundred miles to the eastward, across the Sierra Madres Mountains.

CHAPTER II.

A FIERCE BATTLE WITH APACHE INDIANS, SINGLE HANDED BILLY BONNEY LIBERATES SEGURA FROM JAIL.

In the city of Chihuahua, the two desperadoes led a hurrah life among the sporting elements. Finally their money was gone and their luck at cards went against them. Then Billy and Segura held up and robbed several Monte dealers, when on the way home after their games had closed for the night. One of these Monte dealers had offended Billy, which caused his death.

One morning before the break of day, this Monte dealer was on his way home; a peon was carrying his fat "bank roll" in a buckskin bag, finely decorated with gold and silver threads.

When nearing his residence in the outskirts of the city, Segura and young Bonney made a charge from behind a vacant adobe building. The one-sided battle was soon over. A popular Mexican gambler lay stretched dead on the ground. The peon willingly gave up the sack of gold and silver.

Now towards the Texas border, in a north-easterly direction, a distance of three hundred miles, as fast as their mounts could carry them.

When their horses began to grow tired, other mounts were secured. Their bills were paid enroute, with gold doubloons taken from the buckskin sack.

On reaching the Rio Grande River, which separates Texas from the Republic of Mexico, the young outlaws separated for the time being.

"Billy Bonney finally met up with his Silver City chum, Jesse Evans, and they became partners in crime, in the bordering state of Texas, and the Territories of New Mexico and Arizona. Many robberies and some murders were committed by these smooth-faced boys, and they had many narrow escapes from death, or capture. Fresh horses were always at their command, as they were experts with the lasso, and the scattering ranchmen all had bands of ponies on the range.

Jesse Evans and Unknown

On one occasion the boys ate dinner with a party of Texas emigrants, and were well treated. Leaving the emigrant camp, a band of renegade Apache Indians were seen skulking in the hills. The boys concealed themselves to await results, as they felt sure a raid was to be made on the emigrants, who were headed for the Territory of Arizona. There were only three men in the party, and several women and children.

Just at dusk, the boys, who were stealing along their trail in the low, flint covered hills, heard shooting.

Realizing that a battle was on, Billy Bonney and Jesse Evans put spurs to their mounts and reached the camp just in time.

By this time it was dark. The three men had succeeded in standing off the Indians for awhile, but finally a rush was made on the camp, by the reds, with blood curdling war whoops.

At that moment the two young heroes charged among the Indians and sprang off their horses, with Winchester rifles in hand.

For a few moments the battle raged. One bullet shattered the stock of Billy's rifle, gripping his left hand slightly. He then dropped the rifle and used his pistol.

When the battle was over, eight dead Indians lay on the ground.

The emigrants had shielded themselves by getting behind the wagons. Two of the men were slightly wounded, and the other dangerously shot through the stomach. One little girl had a fractured skull from a blow on the head with a rifle. The mother of the child fainted on seeing her daughter fall.

In telling of this battle, Billy Bonney said the war-whoops shouted by him and Jesse, as they charged into the band of Indians, helped to win the battle. He said a bullet knocked the heel off one of his boots, and that Jesse's hat was shot off his head. He felt sure that the man shot through the stomach died, though he never heard of the party after separating.

Soon after the Indian battle Billy Bonney and Jesse Evans landed in the Mexican village of La Mesilla, New Mexico, and there met up with some of Jesse's chums. Their names were Jim McDaniels, Bill Morton, and Frank Baker.

During their stay in Mesilla, Jim McDaniels christened Billy Bonney, " Billy the Kid," and that name stuck to him to the time of his death.

Finally these three tough cowboys started for the Pecos River with Jesse Evans. "Billy the Kid" promised to join them later, as he had received word that his Old Mexico chum, Segura, was in jail in San Elizario, Texas, below El Paso. This word had been brought by a Mexican boy, sent by Segura.

The "Kid" told the boy to wait in Mesilla till he and Segura got there.

It was the fall of 1876. Mounted on his favorite gray horse, "Billy the Kid" started at six o'clock in the evening for the eighty-one mile ride to San Elizario.

A swift ride brought him into El Paso, then called Franklin, a distance of fifty-six miles, before midnight. Here he dismounted in front of Peter Den's saloon to let his noble "Gray" rest. While waiting, he had a few drinks of whiskey, and fed "Gray" some crackers, there being no horse feed at the saloon.

Now for the twenty-five mile dash down the Rio Grande River, over a level road to San Elizario. It was made in (quick time. Daylight had not yet begun to break.

Dismounting in front of the jail, the "Kid" knocked on the front door. The Mexican jailer asked; "Quien es?" (Who's that?)

The "Kid" replied in good Spanish: "Open up, we have two American prisoners here."

The heavy front door was opened, and the jailer found a cocked pistol pointed at him. Now the frightened guard gave up his pistol and the keys to the cell in which Segura was shackled and handcuffed.

In the rear of the jail building there was another guard asleep. He was relieved of his fire-arms and dagger.

When Segura was free of irons the two guards were gagged so they couldn't give an alarm, and chained to a post.

The two outlaws started out in the darkest part of the night, just before day, Segura on "Gray" and the "Kid" trotting by his side, afoot.

An hour later the two desperadoes were at a confederate's ranch across the Rio Grande River, in Old Mexico.

After filling up with a hot breakfast, the "Kid" was soon asleep, while Segura kept watch for officers. The "Kid's" noble "Gray" was fed and with a mustang, kept hidden out in the brush.

Now the ranchman rode into San Elizario to post himself on the jail break.

Hurrying back to the ranch, he advised his two guests to "hit the high places," as there was great excitement in San Elizario.

Beaching La Mesilla, New Mexico, the two young outlaws found the boy who had carried the message to "Billy the Kid," from Segura, and rewarded him with a handful of Mexican gold.

CHAPTER III.

"BILLY THE KID" AND SEGURA MAKE SUCCESSFUL ROBBERY RAIDS INTO MEXICO. A BATTLE WITH INDIANS, THE "KID" JOINS HIS CHUM, JESSE EVANS.

After a few daring raids into Old Mexico, with Segura, the "Kid" landed in La Mesilla, New Mexico.

Here he fell in with a wild young man by the name of Tom O'Keefe. Together, they started for the Pecos River to meet Jesse Evans and his companions.

Instead of taking the wagon road, the two venturesome boys cut across the Mescalero Apache Indian Reservation, which took in most of the high Guadalupe range of mountains, which separates the Pecos and Rio Grande Rivers.

First they rode into El Paso, Texas, and loaded a pack mule with provisions.

A few days out of El Paso, the boys ran out of water, and were puzzled as to which way to ride.

Finally a fresh Indian trail was found, evidently leading to water. It was followed to the mouth of a deep canyon. For fear of running into a trap, the "Kid" decided to take the canteen and go afoot, leaving his mount and the pack mule with O'Keefe, who was instructed to come to his rescue should he hear yelling and shooting.

A mile of cautious traveling brought the "Kid" to a cool spring of water. The ground was tramped hard with fresh pony and Indian tracks.

After filling the canteen, and drinking all the water he could hold, the "Kid" started down the canyon to join his companion.

He hadn't gone far when Indians, afoot, began pouring out of the cliff to the right, which cut off his retreat down the canyon. There was nothing to do but return towards the spring, as fast as his legs could carry him.

The twenty half-naked braves were gaining on him, and shouting blood-curdling war-whoops.

Like a pursued mountain lion, the "Kid" sprang into the jungles of a steep cliff. Foot by foot his way was made to a place of concealment.

The Indians seeing him leave the trail, scrambled up into the bushy cliff. Now the "Kid's" trusty pistol began to talk, and several young braves, who were leading the chase passed to the "happy hunting ground." The "Kid" said the body of one young buck went down the cliff and caught on the over-hanging limb of a dead tree, and there hung suspended in plain view.

Many shots were fired at the "Kid" when he sprang from one hiding place to another. One bullet struck a rock near his head, and the splinters gave him slight wounds on the face and neck.

Reaching the extreme top of a high peak, the young outlaw felt safe, as he could see no reds on his trail. Being exhausted he soon fell asleep. On hearing the yelling and shooting, Tom O'Keefe stampeded, leaving the "Kid's" mount and the pack mule where they stood.

Reaching a high bluff, which was impossible for a horse to climb, O'Keefe quit his mount and took it afoot. From cliff to cliff, he made his way towards the top of a peak. Finally his keen eyesight caught the figure of a man, far away across a deep canyon, trying to reach the top of a mountain peak. He surmised that the bold climber must be the "Kid."

At last young O'Keefe's strength gave out and he lay down to sleep. His hands and limbs were bleeding from the scratches received from sharp rocks, and he was craving water.

Being refreshed from his long night's sleep, the "Kid" headed for the big red sun, which was just creeping up out of the great "Laino Estacado," (Staked Plains), over a hundred miles to the eastward, across the Pecos River.

Finally water was struck and he was happy. Then he filled up on wild berries, which were plentiful along the borders of the small sparkling stream of water.

Three days later the young hero outlaw reached a cow-camp on the Rio Pecos. He made himself known to the cowboys, who gave him a good horse to ride, and conducted him to the Murphy Dolan cow-camp, where his chum, Jesse Evans, was employed. In this camp the "Kid" also met his former friends, McDaniels, Baker, and Morton.

L. G. Murphy

Here the "Kid" was told of the smoldering cattle war between the Murphy-Dolan faction on one side, and the cattle king, John S. Chisum, on the other.

John S. Chisum

Many small cattle owners were arrayed with the firm of Murphy and Dolan, who owned a large store in Lincoln, and were the owners of many cattle.

On John S. Chisum's side were Alex A. McSween, a prominent lawyer of Lincoln — the County seat of Lincoln County—and a wealthy Englishman by the name of John S. Tunstall, who had only been in America a year.

Alexander McSween

John Tunstall

McSween and Tunstall had formed a co-partnership in the cattle business, and had established a general trading store in Lincoln.

It was now the early spring of 1877. Jesse Evans tried to persuade "Billy the Kid" to join the Murphy-Dolan faction, but he argued that he first had to find Tom O'Keefe, dead or alive, as it was against his principles to desert a chum in time of danger.

For nearly a year a storm had been brewing between John Chisum and the smaller ranchmen. Chisum claimed all the range in the Pecos Valley, from Fort Sumner to the Texas line, a distance of over two hundred miles.

Naturally there was much "mavericking", in other words, stealing unbranded young animals from the Chisum bands of cattle, which ranged about twenty-five miles on each side of the Pecos River.

Chisum owned from forty to sixty thousand cattle on this "Jingle-bob" range. His cattle were marked with a long "Jingle-bob" hanging down from the dew-lap. In branding calves the Chisum cowboys would slash the dewlap above the breast, leaving a chunk of hide and flesh hanging downward. When the wound healed the animal was well marked with a dangling "Jingle-bob." Thus did the Chisum outfit get the name of the "Jingle-bobs."

Well mounted and armed, "Billy the Kid" started in search of Tom O'Keefe. He was found at Las Cruces, three miles from La Mesilla, the County seat of Dona Ana County, New Mexico. It was a happy meeting between the two smooth-faced boys. Each had to relate his experience during and after the Indian trouble.

O'Keefe had gone back to the place where he had left the "Kid's" mount and the pack mule. There he found the "Kid's" horse shot dead, but no sign of the mule. His own pony ran away with the saddle, when he sprang from his back.

Now O'Keefe struck out afoot, towards the west, living on berries and such game as he could kill, finally landing in Las Cruces, where he swore off being the companion of a daring young outlaw.

"Billy the Kid" tried to persuade O'Keefe to accompany him back to the Pecos Valley, to take part in the approaching cattle war, but Tom said he had had enough of playing " bad-man from Bitter Creek."

Now the "Kid" went to a ranch, where he had left his noble "Gray," and with him started back towards the Pecos River.

CHAPTER IV.

THE STARTING OF THE BLOODY LINCOLN COUNTY WAR, THE MURDER OF TUNSTALL, "BILLY THE KID" IS PARTIALLY REVENGED WHEN HE KILLS MORTON AND BAKER.

Arriving back at the Murphy-Dolan cow-camp on the Pecos River, "Billy the Kid" was greeted by his friends, McDaniels, Morton and Baker, who persuaded him to join the Murphy and Dolan outfit, and become one of their fighting cowboys. This he agreed to do, and was put on the pay-roll at good wages.

The summer and fall of 1877 passed along with only now and then a scrap between the factions. But the clouds of war were lowering, and the "Kid" was anxious for a battle.

Still he was not satisfied to be at war with the whole-souled young Englishman, John H. Tunstall, whom he had met on several occasions.

On one of his trips to the Mexican town of Lincoln, to "blow in" his accumulated wages, the "Kid" met Tunstall, and expressed regret at fighting against him.

The matter was talked over and "Billy the Kid" agreed to switch over from the Murphy-Dolan faction. Tunstall at once put him under wages and told him to make his headquarters at their cow-camp on the Rio Feliz, which flowed into the Pecos from the west.

Now the "Kid" rode back to camp and told the dozen cowboys there of his new deal. They tried to persuade him of his mistake, but his mind was made up and couldn't be changed.

In the argument, Baker abused the "Kid" for going back on his friends. This came very near starting a little war in that camp. The "Kid" made Baker back down when he offered to shoot it out with him on the square.

Before riding away on his faithful "Gray," the "Kid" expressed regrets at having to fight against his chum Jesse Evans, in the future.

At the Rio Feliz cow-camp, the "Kid" made friends with all the cowboys there, and with Tunstall and McSween, when he rode into Lincoln to have a good time at the Mexican "fandangos" (dances.)

A few "killings" took place on the Pecos River during the fall, but "Billy the Kid" was not in these fights.

In the early part of December, 1877, the "Kid" received a letter from his Mexican chum whom he had liberated from the jail in San Elizario, Texas, Melquiades Segura, asking that he meet him at their friend's ranch across the Rio Grande River, in Old Mexico, on a matter of great importance.

Mounted on "Gray," the "Kid" started. Meeting Segura, he found that all he wanted was to share a bag of Mexican gold with him.

While visiting Segura, a war started in San Elizario over the Guadalupe Salt Lakes, in El Paso County, Texas.

These Salt Lakes had supplied the natives along the Rio Grande River with free salt for more than a hundred years. An American by the name of Howard, had leased them from the State of Texas, and prohibited the people from taking salt from them.

A prominent man by the name of Louis Cardis took up the fight for the people. Howard and his men were captured and allowed their liberty under the promise that they would leave the Salt Lakes free for the people's use.

Soon after, Howard killed Louis Cardis in El Paso. This worked the natives up to a high pitch.

Under the protection of a band of Texas Rangers, Howard returned to San Elizario, twenty-five miles below El Paso.

On reaching San Elizario the citizens turned out in mass and besieged the Rangers and the Howard crowd, in a house.

Many citizens of Old Mexico, across the river, joined the mob. Among them being Segura and his confederate, at whose ranch "Billy the Kid" and Segura were stopping.

As "Billy the Kid" had no interest in the fight, he took no part, but was an eye witness to it, in the village of San Elizario.

Near the house in which Howard and the Rangers took refuge, lived Captain Gregorio Garcia, and his three sons,

Carlos, Secundio, and Nazean-ceno Garcia. On the roof of their dwelling they constructed a fort, and with rifles, assisted in protecting Howard and the Rangers from the mob.

The fight continued for several days. Finally, against the advice of Captain Gregorio Garcia, the Rangers surrendered. They were escorted up the river towards El Paso, and liberated. Howard, Charlie Ellis, John Atkinson, and perhaps one or two other Americans, were taken out and shot dead by the mob. Thus ended one of the bloody battles which "Billy the Kid" enjoyed as a witness.

The following year the present Governor of New Mexico, Octaviano A. Larrazolo, settled in San Elizario, Texas, and married the pretty daughter of Carlos Garcia, who, with his father and two brothers, so nobly defended Howard and the Rangers.

Now "Billy the Kid," with his pockets bulging with Mexican gold, given him by Segura, returned to the Tunstall-McSween cow camp, on the Rio Feliz, in Lincoln County, New Mexico.

In the month of February, 1878, W. S. Morton, who held a commission as deputy sheriff, raised a posse of fighting cowboys and went to one of the Tunstall cow-camps on the upper Ruidoso River, to attach some horses, which were claimed by the Murphy-Dolan outfit.

Tunstall was at the camp with some of his employees, who "hid out" on the approach of Morton and the posse.

It was claimed by Morton that Tunstall fired the first shot, but that story was not believed by the opposition.

In the fight, Tunstall and his mount were killed. While lying on his face gasping for breath, Tom Hill, who was later killed while robbing a sheep camp, placed a rifle to the back of his head and blew out his brains.

This murder took place on the 18th day of February, 1878.

Before sunset a runner carried the news to "Billy the Kid," on the Rio Feliz. His anger was at the boiling point on hearing of the foul murder. He at once saddled his horse and started to Lincoln, to consult with Lawyer McSween.

Now the Lincoln County war was on with a vengeance and hatred, and the " Kid" was to play a leading hand in it. He swore that he would kill every man who took part in the murder of his friend Tunstall.

At that time, Lincoln County, New Mexico, was the size of some states, about two hundred miles square, and only a few thousand inhabitants, mostly Mexicans, scattered over its surface.

On reaching the town of Lincoln, the "Kid" was informed by McSween that R. M. Brewer (Brewer) had been sworn in as a special constable, and was making up a posse to arrest the murderers of Tunstall.

"Billy the Kid" joined the Brewer posse, and they started for the Rio Pecos River.

On the 6th day of March, the Brewer posse ran onto five mounted men at the lower crossing of the Rio Penasco, six miles from the Pecos River. They fled and were pursued by Brewer and his crowd.

Two of the fleeing cowboys separated from their companions. The "Kid" recognized them as Morton and Baker, his former friends. He dashed after them, and the rest of the posse followed his lead.

Shots were being fired back and forth. At last Morton's and Baker's mounts fell over dead. The two men then crawled into a sink-hole to shield their bodies from the bullets.

A parley was held, and the two men surrendered, after Brewer had promised them protection. The "Kid" protested against giving this pledge. He remarked: "My time will come."

Now the posse started for the Chisum home ranch, on South Spring River, with the two handcuffed prisoners.

On the morning of the 9th day of March, the Brewer posse started with the prisoners for Lincoln, but pretended to be headed for Fort Sumner.

The posse was made up of the following men: R. M. Brewer, J. G. Scurlock, Charlie Bowdre, "Billy the Kid," Henry Brown, Frank McNab, Fred Wayt, Sam Smith, Jim French, John Middleton and McClosky.

Richard M. Brewer

After traveling five miles they came to the little village of Roswell. Here they stopped to allow Morton time to write a letter to his cousin, the Hon. H. H. Marshall, of Richmond, Virginia.

Ash Upson was the postmaster in Roswell and Morton asked him to notify his cousin in Virginia if the posse failed to keep their pledge of protection.

McClosky, who was standing near, remarked: "If harm comes to you two, they will have to kill me first."

The party started out about 10 A. M. from Roswell. About 4 P. M., Martin Chavez of Picacho, arrived in Roswell and reported to Ash Upson that the posse and their prisoners had quit the main road to Lincoln and had turned off in the direction of Agua Negra, an unfrequented watering place. This move satisfied the postmaster that the doom of Morton and Baker was sealed.

On March the eleventh, Frank McNab, one of the Brewer posse, rode up to the post-office and dismounted. Mr. Upson expressed surprise and told him that he supposed he was in Lincoln by this time. Now McNab confessed that Morton, Baker and McClosky were dead.

Later, Ash Upson got the particulars from "Billy the Kid" of the killing.

The "Kid" and Charlie Bowdre were riding in the lead as they neared Blackwater Spring. McClosky and Middleton rode by the side of the two prisoners. The balance of the posse followed behind.

Finally Brown and McNab spurred up their horses and rode up to McClosky and Middleton. McNab shoved a cocked pistol at McClosky's head saying: "You are the s—of a b— that's got to die before harm can come to these fellows, are you?"

Now the trigger was pulled and McClosky fell from his horse, dead, shot through the head.

"Billy the Kid" heard the shot and wheeled his horse around in time to see the two prisoners dashing away on their mounts. The "Kid" fired twice and Morton and Baker fell from their horses, dead. No doubt it was a put up job to allow the "Kid" to kill the murderers of his friend Tunstall, with his own hands.

The posse rode on to Lincoln, all but McNab, who returned to Roswell. The bodies of McClosky, Morton and Baker were left where they fell. Later they were buried by some sheep herders.

Thus ends the first chapter of the bloody Lincoln County war.

Frank McNab

CHAPTER V.

THE MURDER OF SHERIFF BRADY AND HIS DEPUTY HINDMAN BY THE "KID" AND HIS BAND, "BILLY THE KID" AND JESSE EVANS MEET AS ENEMIES AND PART AS FRIENDS.

On returning to Lincoln, "Billy the Kid" had many consultations with Lawyer McSween about the murder of Tunstall. It was agreed to never let up until all the murderers were in their graves.

The "Kid" heard that one of Tunstall's murderers was seen around Dr. Blazer's saw mill, near the Mescalero Apache Indian Reservation, on South Fork, about forty miles from Lincoln. He at once notified Officer Dick Brewer, who made up a posse to search for Roberts, an ex-soldier, a fine rider, and a dead shot.

As the posse rode up to Blazer's saw mill from the east, Roberts came galloping up from the west. The "Kid" put spurs to his horse and made a dash at him. Both had pulled their Winchester rifles from the scabbards. Both men fired at the same time, Robert's bullet went whizzing past the "Kid's" ear, while the one from "Billy the Kid's" rifle found lodgment in Robert's body. It was a death wound, but gave Roberts time to prove his bravery, and fine marksmanship.

He fell from his mount and found concealment in an outhouse, from where he fought his last battle.

The posse men dismounted and found concealment behind the many large saw logs, scattered over the ground.

For a short time the battle raged, while the lifeblood was fast flowing from Robert's wound. One of his bullets struck Charlie Bowdre, giving him a serious wound. Another bullet cut off a finger from George Coe's hand. Still another went crashing through Dick Brewer's head, as he peeped over a log to get a shot at Roberts; Brewer fell over dead. This was Robert's last shot, as he soon expired from the wound "Billy the Kid" had given him.

George Coe

A grave yard was now started on a round hill near the Blazer saw mill, and in later years, Mr. and Mrs. George Nesbeth, a little girl, and a strange man, who had died with their boots on—being foully murdered were buried in this miniature "Boot Hill" cemetery.

Two of the participants in the battle at Blazer's saw mill, Frank and George Coe, are still alive, being highly respected ranchmen on the Ruidoso River, where both have raised large families.

After the battle at Blazer's mill, the Coe brothers joined issues with "Billy the Kid" and fought other battles against the Murphy-Dolan faction. In one battle Frank Coe was arrested and taken to the Lincoln jail. Through the aid of friends he made his escape.

Now that their lawful leader, Dick Brewer, was in his grave, the posse returned to Lincoln. Here they formed themselves into a band, without lawful authority, to avenge the murder of Tunstall, until not one was left alive. By common consent, "Billy the Kid" was appointed their leader.

In Lincoln, lived one of "Billy the Kid's" enemies, J. B. Mathews, known as Billy Mathews. While he had taken no part in the killing of Tunstall, he had openly expressed himself in favor of Jimmie Dolan and Murphy, and against the other faction.

Frank Coe

On the 28th day of March, Billy Mathews, unarmed, met the "Kid" on the street by accident. Mathews started into a doorway, just as the "Kid" cut down on him with a rifle. The bullet shattered the door frame above his head.

Major William Brady, a brave and honest man, was the sheriff of Lincoln County. He was partial to the Murphy-Dolan faction, and this offended the opposition. He held warrants for "Billy the Kid" and his associates, for the killing of Morton, Baker, and Roberts.

On the first day of April, 1878, Sheriff Brady left the Murphy-Dolan store, accompanied by George Hindman and J. B. Mathews to go to the Court House and announce that no term of court would be held at the regular April term.

The sheriff and his two companions carried rifles in their hands, as in those days every male citizen who had grown to manhood, went well armed.

The Tunstall and McSween store stood about midway between the Murphy-Dolan store and the Court House.

In the rear of the Tunstall-McSween store, there was an adobe corral, the east side of which projected beyond the store building, and commanded a view of the street, over which the sheriff had to pass. On the top of this corral wall, "Billy the Kid" and his "warriors" had cut grooves in which to rest their rifles.

As the sheriff and party came in sight, a volley was fired at them from the adobe fence. Brady and Hindman fell mortally wounded, and Mathews found shelter behind a house on the south side of the street.

Sheriff William Brady

Ike Stockton, who afterwards became a killer of men, and a bold desperado, in northwestern New Mexico, and southwestern Colorado, and who was killed in Durango, Colorado, at that time kept a saloon in Lincoln, and was a friend of the "Kid's." He ran out of his saloon to the wounded officers. Hindman called for water; Stockton ran to the Bonita River, nearby, and brought him a drink in his hat.

Isaac "Ike" and Amanda Stockton

About this time, "Billy the Kid" leaped over the adobe wall and ran to the fallen officers. As he raised Sheriff Brady's rifle from the ground, J. B. Mathews fired at him from his hiding place. The ball shattered the stock of the sheriff's rifle and plowed a furrow through the "Kid's" side, but it proved not to be a dangerous wound.

Now "Billy the Kid" broke for shelter at the McSween home. Some say that he fired a parting shot into Sheriff Brady's head. Others dispute it. At any rate both Brady and Hindman lay dead on the main street of Lincoln.

This cold-blooded murder angered many citizens of Lincoln against the "Kid" and his crowd. Now they became outlaws in every sense of the word.

From now on the " Kid" and his " warriors" made their headquarters at McSween's residence, when not scouting over the country searching for enemies, who sanctioned the killing of Tunstall.

Often this little band of "warriors" would ride through the streets of Lincoln to defy their enemies, and be royally treated by their friends.

Finally, George W. Pepin was appointed Sheriff of the County, and he appointed a dozen or more deputies to help uphold the law. Still bloodshed and anarchy continued throughout the County, as the "Kid's" crowd was not idle.

San Patricio, a Mexican plaza on the Ruidoso River, about eight miles below Lincoln, was a favorite hangout for the "Kid" and his "warriors," as most of the natives there were their sympathizers.

One morning, before breakfast, in San Patricio, Jose Miguel Sedillo brought the "Kid" news that Jesse Evans and a crowd of " Seven River Warriors" were prowling around in the hills, near the old Brewer ranch, where a band of the Chisum-McSween horses were being kept.

Thinking that their intentions were to steal these horses, the "Kid" and party started without eating breakfast. In the party, besides the "Kid," were Charlie Bowdre, Henry Brown, J. G. Scurlock, John Middleton, and a young Texan by the name of Tom O'Folliard, who had lately joined the gang.

Henry Brown

On reaching the hills, the party split, the "Kid" taking Henry Brown with him.

Soon the "Kid" heard shooting in the direction taken by the balance of his party. Putting spurs to his mount, he dashed up to Jesse Evans and four of his "warriors," who had captured Charlie Bowdre, and was joking with him about his leader, the "Kid." He remarked: "We are hungry, and thought we would roast the 'Kid' for breakfast. We want to hear him bleat."

At that moment a horseman dashed up among them from an arroyo. With a smile, Charlie Bowdre said, pointing at the "Kid;" "There comes your breakfast, Jesse!"

With drawn pistol, "Old Gray" was checked up in front of his former chum in crime, Jesse Evans.

With a smile, Jesse remarked: "Well, Billy, this is a hell of a way to introduce yourself to a private picnic party."

The "Kid" replied, "How are you, Jesse? It's a long time since we met."

Jesse said: "I understand you are after the men who killed that Englishman. I, nor none of my men were there."

"I know you wasn't, Jesse," replied the "Kid." "If you had been, the ball would have been opened before now."

Soon the "Kid" was joined by the rest of his party and both bands separated in peace.

CHAPTER VI.

"BILLY THE KID" AND GANG STAND OFF A POSSE AT THE CHISUM RANCH, A BLOODY BATTLE IN LINCOLN WHICH LASTED THREE DAYS.

As time went on, Sheriff Peppin appointed new deputies on whom he could depend. Among these being Marion Turner of the firm of Turner & Jones, merchants at Roswell on the Pecos River.

For several years, Turner had been employed by cattle king John Chisum, and up to May, 1878 had helped to fight his battles, but for some reason he had seceded and became Chisum's bitter enemy.

Marion Turner was put in charge of the Sheriff's forces in the Pecos Valley, and soon had about forty daring cowboys and cattlemen under his command. Roswell was their headquarters.

Early in July, "Billy the Kid" and fourteen of his followers rode up to the Chisum headquarters ranch, five miles from Roswell, to make that their rendezvous.

Turner with his force tried to oust the "Kid" and gang from their stronghold, but found it impossible, owing to the house being built like a fort to stand off Indians, but he kept out spies to catch the "Kid" napping.

One morning, Turner received word that the "Kid" and party had left for Fort Sumner on the upper Pecos River. The trail was followed about twenty miles up the river, where it switched off towards Lincoln, a distance of about eighty or ninety miles.

The trail was followed to Lincoln, where it was found that "Billy the Kid" and gang had taken possession of McSween's fine eleven-room residence, and were prepared to stand off an army.

On arriving in Lincoln with his posse, Turner was joined by Sheriff Peppin and his deputies, and they made the "Big House," as the Murphy-Dolan store was called, their headquarters.

For three days shots were fired back and forth from the buildings, which were far apart.

On the morning of July 19th, 1878, Marion Turner concluded to take some of his men to the McSween residence and demand the surrender of the "Kid" and his "warriors." With Turner were his business partner, John A. Jones and eight other fearless men.

At that moment the "Kid" and party were in a rear room holding a consultation, otherwise some of the advancing party might have been killed.

On reaching the thick adobe wall of the building, through which portholes had been cut, Turner and his men found protection against the wall between these openings.

When the "Kid" and party returned to the port-holes they were hailed by Turner, who demanded their surrender, as he had warrants for their arrest.

The "Kid" replied: "We, too, hold warrants for you and your gang, which we will serve on you, hot from the muzzles of our guns."

About this time Lieut. Col. Dudley, of the Ninth Cavalry, arrived from Ft. Stanton with a company of infantry and some artillery.

Planting his cannons midway between the belligerent parties, Col. Dudley proclaimed that he would turn his guns loose on the first of the two, who fired over the heads of his command.

Despite this warning, shots were fired back and forth, but no harm was done.

Now Martin Chavez, who at this writing is a prosperous merchant in Santa Fe, rode up with thirty-five Mexicans, whom he had deputized to protect McSween and the "Kid's" party.

Col. Dudley asked him under what authority he was acting. He replied that he held a certificate as deputy sheriff under Brady. Col. Dudley told him that as Sheriff Brady was dead, and a new sheriff had been appointed, his commission was not in effect. Still he proclaimed that he would protect the "Kid" and McSween.

Now Col. Dudley ordered Chavez off the field of battle, or he would have his men fire on them. When the guns were pointed in their direction, the Chavez crowd retreated to the Ellis Hotel. Here he ordered his followers to fire on the soldiers if they opened up on the "Kid" and party with their cannon.

Toward night the Turner men, who were up against the McSween residence, between the port-holes, managed to set fire to the front door and windows. A strong wind carried the blaze to the woodwork of other rooms.

Mrs. McSween and her three lady friends had left the building before the fight started. She had made one trip back to see her husband. The firing ceased while she was in the house.

Mrs. Susan McSween

In the front parlor, Mrs. McSween had a fine piano. To prevent it from burning, the "Kid" moved it from one room to another until it was finally in the kitchen.

The crowd made merry around the piano, singing and "pawing the ivory," as the "Kid" expressed it to the writer a few months later.

After dark, when the fiery flames began to lick their way into the kitchen, where the smoke begrimed band were congregated, a question of surrender was discussed, but the

"Kid" put his veto on the move. He stood near the outer door of the kitchen, with his rifle, and swore he would kill the first man who cried surrender. He had planned to wait until the last minute, then all rush out of the door together, and make a run for the Bonita River, a distance of about fifty yards.

Finally the heat became so great; the kitchen door was thrown open.

At this moment one Mexican became frightened and called out at the top of his voice not to shoot, that they would surrender. The "Kid" struck the fellow over the head with his rifle and knocked him senseless.

When the Mexican called out that they would surrender, Robert W. Beckwith, a cattleman of Seven Rivers, and John Jones, stepped around the corner of the building in full view of the kitchen door.

Robert W. Beckwith

A shot was fired at Beckwith and wounded him on the hand. Then Beckwith opened fire and shot Lawyer McSween, though this was not a death shot. Another shot from Beckwith's gun killed Vicente Romero. Now the "Kid" planted a bullet in Beckwith's head, and he fell over dead. Leaping over Beckwith's body, the band made a run for the river. The "Kid" was in the lead yelling: "Come on, boys!" Tom O'Folliard was in the rear. He made his escape amidst flying bullets, without a scratch, although he had stopped to pick up his friend Harvey Morris. Finding him dead he dropped the body.

McSween fell dead in the back yard with nine bullets in his body, which was badly scorched by the fire, before he left the building.

It was 10 P. M. when the fight had ended. Seven men had been killed and many wounded. Only two of Turner's posse were killed, while the "Kid" lost five,—McSween, Morris and three Mexicans.

CHAPTER VII.

"BILLY THE KID" KILLS TWO MORE MEN. AT THE HEAD OF A RECKLESS BAND, HE STEALS HORSES BY THE WHOLESALE. HE BECOMES DESPERATELY IN LOVE WITH MISS DULCINEA DEL TOBOSO.

After their escape from Lincoln, "Billy the Kid" got his little band together, and made a business of stealing stock and gambling. Their headquarters were made in the hills near Fort Stanton—only a few miles above Lincoln. The soldiers at the Fort paid no attention to them.

Now Governor Lew Wallace, the famous author of "Ben Hur," of Santa Fe, the capital of the Territory of New Mexico, issued a proclamation granting a pardon to "Billy the Kid" and his followers, if they would quit their lawlessness, but the "Kid" laughed it off as a joke.

Lew Wallace

On the 5th day of August, "Billy the Kid" and gang rode up in plain view of the Mescalero Indian Agency and began rounding up a band of horses.

A Jew by the name of Bernstein, mounted a horse and said he would go out and stop them. He was warned of the danger, but persisted in his purpose of preventing the stealing of their band of gentle saddle horses.

When Mr. Bernstein rode up to the gang and told them to "vamoose," in other words, to hit the road, the "Kid" drew his rifle and shot the poor Jew dead. This was the "Kid's" most cowardly act. His excuse was that he "didn't like a Jew, no-how."

During the fall the government had given a contract to a large gang of Mexicans to put up several hundred tons of hay at $25 a ton. As they drew their pay, the "Kid" and gang were on hand to deal Monte and win their money.

When the contract was finished, there was no more business for the "Kid's" Monte game, so with his own hand, as told to the author by himself, he set fire to the hay stacks one windy night.

Now the Government gave another contract for several hundred tons of hay at $50 a ton—as the work had to be rushed before frost killed the grass.

When pay day came around the "Kid's" Monte game was raking in money again.

The new stacks were allowed to stand, as it was too late in the season to cut the grass for more hay.

During the fall the "Kid" and some of his gang made trips to Fort Sumner. Bowdre and Scurlock always remained near their wives in Lincoln, but finally those two outlaws moved their families to "Sumner," where a rendezvous was established. Here one of their gang, who always kept in the dark and worked on the sly, lived with his Mexican wife, a sister to the wife of Pat Garrett. His name was Barney Mason, and he carried a curse of God on his brow for the killing of John Farris, a cowboy friend of the writer's, in the early winter of 1878.

Joshia G. "Doc" Scurlock

On one of his trips to Fort Sumner, "Billy the Kid" fell desperately in love with a pretty little seventeen-year-old half-breed Mexican girl, whom we will call Miss Dulcinea del Toboso. She was a daughter of a once famous man, and a sister to a man who owned sheep on a thousand hills. The falling in love with this pretty, young miss was virtually the cause of "Billy the Kid's" death, as up to the last he hovered around Fort Sumner like a moth around a blazing candle. He had no thought of getting his wings singed; he couldn't resist the temptation of visiting this pretty little miss.

During the month of September, 1878, the "Kid" and part of his gang visited the town of Lincoln, and on leaving there stole a large band of fine range horses from Charlie Fritz and others.

This band of horses was driven to Fort Sumner, thence east to Tascosa in the wild Panhandle of Texas, on the Canadian River.

While disposing of these horses to the cattlemen and cowboys, the "Kid" and his gang camped for several weeks at the "LX" cattle ranch, twenty miles below Tascosa.

It was here, during the months of October and November, 1878, that the writer made the acquaintance of "Billy the

Kid," Tom O'Folliard, Henry Brown, Fred Wyat, John Middleton, and others of the gang whose names can't be recalled.

The author had just returned from Chicago where he had taken a shipment of fat steers, and found this gang of outlaws camped under some large cottonwood trees, within a few hundred yards of the "LX" headquarter ranch house.

For a few weeks, much of my time was spent with "Billy the Kid." We became quite chummy. He presented me with a nicely bound book, in which he wrote his autograph. I had previously given him a fine meerschaum cigar holder.

While loafing in their camp, we passed off the time playing cards and shooting at marks. With our Colt's 45 pistols I could hit the mark as often as the "Bad," but when it came to quick shooting, he could get in two shots to my one.

I found "Billy the Kid" to be a good natured young man. He was always cheerful and smiling. Being still in his teens, he had no sign of a beard. His eyes were a hazel blue, and his brown hair was long and curly. The skin on his face was tanned to a chestnut brown, and was as soft and tender as a baby's. He weighed about one hundred and forty pounds, and was five feet, eight inches tall. His only defects were two upper front teeth, which projected outward from his well shaped mouth.

During his many visits to Tascosa, where whiskey was plentiful, the "Kid" never got drunk. He seemed to drink more for sociability than for the "love of liquor."

Here Henry Brown and Fred Wyat quit the "Kid's" outlaw gang and went to the Chickasaw Nation, in the Indian Territory, where the parents of half-breed Fred Wyat lived.

It is said that Fred Wyat, in later years, served as a member of the Oklahoma Legislature.

Henry Brown became City Marshal of Caldwell, Kansas, and while wearing his star rode to the nearby town of Medicine Lodge, with three companions and in broad day light, held up the bank, killing the president, Wiley Payne, and his cashier, George Jeppert. This put an end to Henry Brown, as the enraged citizens mobbed the whole band of "bad men."

The snow had begun to fly when the "Kid" and the remnant of his gang returned to Fort Sumner, New Mexico.

One of his followers, John Middleton, had sworn off being an outlaw and rode away from Tascosa, for southern Kansas, where the author met him in later years. He had settled down to a peaceful life.

John Middleton

The "Kid" made his headquarters at Fort Sumner, so as to be near his sweetheart. He made several raids into Lincoln County to steal cattle and horses. On one of these trips to Lincoln County, his respect for women and children, avoided a bloody battle with United States soldiers.

In the month of February, 1879, Wm. H. McBroom, at the head of a United States surveying crew, established a camp at the Roberts ranch on the Penasco Creek, in the Pecos Valley.

While absent with most of his crew, Mr. McBroom left a young man, twenty-two years of age, Will M. Tipton, in charge of the camp and extra mules. A young Mexican by the name of Nicholas Gutierrez was detailed to help young Tipton care for the stock.

Their camp was within a few hundred feet of the Roberts home, on the bank of the creek. One morning Mr. Roberts started up the river to Roswell to buy supplies, leaving his wife, grown daughter, and five-year-old son at the ranch.

Later that evening, Captain Hooker and some Negro soldiers pitched camp near the Roberts home. They had several American prisoners with them, to be taken to Fort Stanton and placed in jail.

That night after supper, Mr. Will M. Tipton, who at this writing, 1920, is a highly respected citizen of Santa Fe, New Mexico, says he and Nicolas Gutierrez were sitting on the bank of the creek in their camp. He was playing a guitar while Nicolas was singing. Just then a horseman climbed up the steep embankment from the bed of the creek, and dismounted.

This stranger began asking questions about the soldiers' camp, where the camp-fires blazed brilliantly in the pitchy darkness.

Finally the stranger gave a shrill whistle, and soon a companion rode into camp, out of the bed of the creek.

This second visitor was a slender, boyish young man, who seemed anxious to learn all about the soldiers' camp.

In a few moments three Negro soldiers strolled into camp and chatted awhile. When they left to return to their quarters, the two strangers bade Tipton and his companion goodnight, and rode down the bed of the creek.

At noon next day, Mr. Roberts returned from Roswell. On meeting young Tipton, he remarked: "You boys had 'Billy the Kid' as a visitor last night." He then told of meeting the "Kid" and his band of "warriors" that morning, and of how the "Kid" told of his visit to the McBroom camp. He told Will Tipton that the small young man was the "Kid."

"Billy the Kid" had told Roberts that they had planned to make a charge into the soldiers' camp and liberate the prisoners, who were friends of theirs, but finding that Mrs. Roberts and the children were alone, and that the soldiers' camp was so near the Roberts home, they gave up the proposed battle, knowing that the shooting would disturb Mrs. Roberts and the family.

Mr. Roberts explained to Mr. Tipton that he had always fed the "Kid" and his "warriors" when they happened by his place, hence their friendship for him.

Now the "Kid" and his party rode to Lincoln to use their influence in a peaceful way to liberate their friends, whom Capt. Hooker intended to turn over to the new sheriff of Lincoln County.

In Lincoln the "Kid" met his former chum, Jesse Evans, and they started out to celebrate the meeting. With Jesse Evans was a desperado named William Campbell.

One night a lawyer named Chapman, who had been sent from Las Vegas to settle up the McSween estate, was in the saloon, when Campbell shot at his feet to make him dance. The lawyer protested indignantly and was shot dead by Campbell. Jimmie Dolan and J. B. Mathews, being present, were later arrested, along with Campbell, for this killing.

Dolan and Mathews came clear at the preliminary trial, and Campbell was bound over to the Grand Jury. He was taken to Fort Stanton and placed in jail. There he made his escape and has never been heard of in that part of the country since.

James (Jimmie) Dolan

Now "Billy the Kid" and Tom O'Folliard rode back to Fort Sumner, but soon returned to Lincoln, where they were arrested by Sheriff Kimball and his deputies—merely as a matter of performing their duty, but with no intention of disgracing them. They were turned over to Deputy Sheriff T. B. Longworth and guarded in the home of Don Juan Patron, where they were wined and dined.

On the 21st day of March, 1879, Deputy Sheriff Longworth received orders to place his two prisoners in the town jail—a filthy hole.

Arriving at the jail door, the "Kid" told Mr. Longworth that he had been in this jail once before, and he swore he would never go into it again, but to avoid making trouble, he would go back on his pledge.

On a pine door to one of the cells, the "Kid" wrote with his pencil: "William Bonney was incarcerated first time, December 22nd, 1878 — Second time, March 21st, 1879, and hope I will never be again. W. H. Bonney."

This inscription showed on the old jail door for many years after it was written.

The first time the "Kid" was put in this jail he walked right out, and this second time, he broke down the door when he got ready to go.

After breaking out of the jail, the "Kid" and O'Folliard spent a couple of weeks in Lincoln, carrying their rifles whenever they walked through the street, in plain view of the sheriff.

In April, they returned to Fort Sumner and were joined by Charlie Bowdre and Scurlock. Jesse Evans had left for the lower Pecos, where he was later killed, according to reports.

Charlie Bowdre

The summer was spent by the "Kid" and his followers stealing cattle and horses.

In October they went to Roswell and stole 118 head of John Chisum's fattest steers, and later sold them to Colorado beef buyers. The "Kid" claimed that Chisum owed him for fighting his battles during the Lincoln County war, and he was using this method to get his pay.

From now on, for the next year, the "Kid" and gang did a wholesale business in stealing cattle. Tom Cooper and his gang had joined issues with the "Kid" and party, and they established headquarters at the Portales Lake — a salty body of water at the foot of the Staked Plains, about seventy-five miles east of Fort Sumner.

Here a permanent camp was pitched against a cliff of rock, at a fresh water spring, and it afterward became noted as "Billy the Kid's" cave. A rock wall had been built against the cliff to take in the spring, and afforded protection as a fort in case of a surprise from Indians or law-officers.

They had the whole country to themselves, as there were no inhabitants— only drifting bands of buffalo hunters.

Raids were made into the Texas Panhandle, the western line being a few miles east of their camp, and fat steers stolen from the "LX" and "LIT" cattle ranges on the Canadian river.

These herds of stolen steers were driven to Tularosa, in Dona Ana County, New Mexico, and turned over to Pat Cohglin, the "King of Tularosa," who had a contract to furnish beef to the U. S. soldiers at Ft. Stanton. Cohglin had made a deal with "Billy the Kid" to buy all the steers he could steal in the Texas Panhandle, and deliver to him in Tularosa.

In January, 1880, the "Kid" added another notch on the handle of his pistol as a man-killer. He and a crowd of the Chisum cowboys were celebrating in Bob Hargroves' saloon in Fort Sumner. A bad-man from Texas, by the name of Joe Grant, was filling his hide full of "Kill-me-quick" whiskey, in the Hargroves' saloon.

Grant pulled a fine, ivory-handled Colt's pistol from the scabbard of Cowboy Finan, putting his own pistol in place of it.

Here the "Kid" asked Grant to let him look at this beautiful, ivory-handled pistol. The request was granted. Then the "Kid" revolved the cylinder and saw there were two empty chambers. He let the hammer down so that the first two attempts to shoot would be failures.

Now the pretty pistol was handed back to Grant and he stuck it in his scabbard.

A little later Grant stepped behind the bar, so as to face the crowd, and jerking his pistol, he began knocking glasses off the bar with it. Eyeing "Billy the Kid," he remarked: "Pard, I'll kill a man quicker than you will, for the whiskey."

The "Kid" accepted the challenge. Grant fired at the "Kid," but the hammer struck on an empty chamber. Now the "Kid" planted a ball between Grant's eyes and he fell over dead.

At the Bosque Grande, on the Pecos River, the three Dedrick boys, Sam, Dan, and Mose, owned a ranch, which became quite a rendezvous for the "Kid's" and Tom Cooper's gangs. From here the herds of stolen Panhandle, Texas, cattie were started across the waterless desert to the foot of the Capitan mountains, a distance of about one hundred miles.

Here Dave Rudabaugh, who had the previous fall killed the jailer in Las Vegas in trying to liberate his friend, Webb, joined "Billy the Kid's" gang. Also Billy Wilson and Tom Pickett joined the party, and their time was spent stealing cattle and horses.

CHAPTER VIII.

"BILLY THE KID" ADDS ONE MORE NOTCH TO HIS GUN AS A KILLER, TRAPPED AT LAST BY PAT GARRETT AND POSSE, TWO OF HIS GANG KILLED, IN JAIL AT SANTA FE.

In the year 1879, rich gold ore had been struck on Baxter Mountain, three miles from White Oaks Spring, about thirty miles north of Lincoln, and the new town of White Oaks was established, with a population of about one thousand souls.

The "Kid" had many friends in this hurrah mining camp. He had shot up the town, and was wanted by the law officers.

On the 23rd day of November, 1880, the "Kid" celebrated his birthday in White Oaks, under cover, among friends.

On riding out of town with his gang after dark, he took one friendly shot at Deputy Sheriff Jim Woodland, who was standing in front of the Pioneer Saloon. The chances are he had no intention of shooting Woodland, as he was a warm friend to his chum, Tom O'Folliard, who was riding by his side. O'Folliard and Jim Woodland had come to New Mexico from Texas together, a few years previous. Woodland is still a resident of Lincoln County, with a permanent home on the large Block cattle ranch.

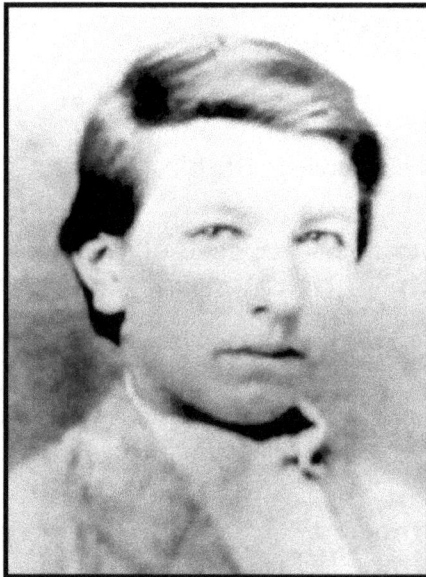

Tom O'Folliard

This shot woke up Deputy Sheriffs Jim Carlyle and J. W. Bell, who fired parting shots at the gang, as they galloped out of town.

The next day a posse was made up of leading citizens of White Oaks with Deputy Sheriff Will Hudgens and Jim Carlyle in command. They followed the trail of the outlaw gang to Coyote Spring, where they came onto the gang in camp. Shots were exchanged, "Billy the Kid" had sprung onto his horse, which was shot from under him.

When the "Kid's" gang fired on the posse, Johnny Hudgens' mount fell over dead, shot in the head.

The weather was bitter cold and snow lay on the ground. Without overcoat or gloves, "Billy the Kid" rushed for the hills, afoot, after his horse fell. The rest of the gang had become separated, and each one looked out for himself.

In the outlaws' camp the posse found a good supply of grub and plunder.

Jim Carlyle appropriated the "Kid's" gloves and put them on his hands. No doubt they were the real cause of his death later.

With "Billy the Kid's" saddle, overcoat and the other plunder found in the outlaws' camp, the posse returned to White Oaks, arriving there about dark.

It would seem from all accounts that "Billy the Kid" trailed the posse into White Oaks, where he found shelter at the Dedrick and West Livery Stable. He was seen on the street during the night.

On November 27th, a posse of White Oaks citizens under command of Jim Carlyle and Will Hudgens, rode to the Jim Greathouse road-ranch, about forty miles north, arriving there before daylight. Their horses were secreted, and they made breastworks of logs and brush, so as to cover the ranch house, which was known to be a rendezvous of the "Kid's" gang.

After daylight the cook came out of the house with a nosebag and ropes to hunt the horses which had been hobbled the evening before.

This cook, Steck, was captured by the posse behind the breastworks. He confessed that the "Kid" and his gang were in the house.

Now Steck was sent to the house with a note to the "Kid" demanding his surrender. The reply he sent back by Steck read: "You can only take me a corpse."

The proprietor of the ranch, Jim Greathouse, accompanied Steck back to the posse behind the logs.

Jimmie Carlyle suggested that he go to the house unarmed and have a talk with the "Kid." Will Hudgens wouldn't agree to this until after Greathouse said he would remain to guarantee Carlyle's safe return and that if the "Kid" should kill Carlyle, they could take his life.

A time limit was set for Carlyle's return, or Greathouse would be killed. This was written on a note and sent by Steck to the "Kid."

When Carlyle entered the saloon, in the front part of the log building, the "Kid" greeted him in a friendly manner, but seeing his gloves sticking out of Carlyle's coat pocket, he grabbed them, saying: "What in the h—l are you doing with my gloves?" Of course this brought back the misery he had endured without gloves after the posse raided their camp at Coyote Spring.

Here he invited Carlyle up to the bar to take his last drink on earth—as he said he intended to kill him when the whiskey was down.

After Carlyle had drained his glass the "Kid" pulled his pistol and told him to say his prayers before he fired.

With a laugh the "Kid" put up his pistol, saying, "Why, Jimmie, I wouldn't kill you. Let's all take another friendly drink."

Now the time was spent singing and dancing. Every time the gang took a drink, Carlyle had to join them in a social glass.

The "Kid" afterwards told friends that he had no intention of killing Carlyle and that he just wanted to detain him till after dark, so they could make a dash for liberty.

The time had just expired when the posse was to kill Jim Greathouse, if Carlyle was not back. At that moment a man behind the breastworks fired a shot at the house. Carlyle supposed this shot had killed Greathouse, which would result in his own death. He leaped for the glass window, taking sash and all with him. The " Kid" fired a bullet into him. When he struck the ground he began crawling away on his hands and knees, as he was badly wounded. Now the "Kid" finished him with a well aimed shot from his pistol.

The men behind the logs were witnesses to this murder,— as they could see Carlyle crawling away from the window. Now they opened fire with a vengeance on the building. The gang had previously piled sacks of grain and flour against the doors, to keep out the bullets.

In the excitement, Jim Greathouse slipped away from the posse and ran through the woods. Finding one of his own hobbled ponies, he mounted him and rode away. He was later shot by desperado Joe Fowler, with a double-barrel shot gun, as he lay in bed asleep. This murder took place on Joe Fowler's cattle ranch west of Socorro, New Mexico.

After dark the posse concluded to return to White Oaks, as they were cold and hungry. They had brought no grub with them, and they dared not build a fire to keep warm, for fear of being shot by the gang.

A few hours later the "Kid" and gang made a break for liberty, intending to fight the posse to a finish, they not knowing that the officers had departed.

All night the gang waded through the deep snow, afoot. They arrived at Mr. Spence's ranch at daylight, and ate a hearty breakfast. Then continued their journey towards Anton Chico on the Pecos River.

About daylight that morning, Will Hudgens, Johnny Hurley, and Jim Brent made up a large posse and started to the Greathouse road-ranch. Arriving there, they found the place vacated. The buildings were set afire, and then the journey continued on the gang's trail, in the deep snow.

A highly respected citizen, by the name of Spence, had established a road ranch on a cut-off road between White

Oaks and Las Vegas. The gang's trail led up to this ranch, and Mr. Spence acknowledged coking breakfast for them.

Now Mr. Spence was dragged to a tree with a rope around his neck to hang him. Many of the posse protested against the hanging of Spence, and his life was spared, but revenge was taken by burning up his buildings.

The "Kid's" trail was now followed into a rough, hilly country and there abandoned. Then the posse returned to White Oaks.

In Anton Chico, the "Kid" and his party stole horses and saddles, and rode down the Pecos River.

A few days later, Pat Garrett, the sheriff of Lincoln County, arrived in Anton Chico from Fort Sumner, to make up a posse to run down the "Kid" and his gang.

Patrick Floyd Garrett

At this time the writer and Bob Roberson had arrived in Anton Chico from Tascosa, Texas, with a crew of fighting cowboys, to help run down the "Kid," and put a stop to the stealing of Panhandle, Texas, cattle.

The author had charge of five "warriors," Jas. H. East, Cal Polk, Lee Hall, Frank Clifford (Big-Foot Wallace), and Lon Chambers. We were armed to the teeth, and had four large mules to draw the mess-wagon, driven by the Mexican cook, Francisco.

Bob Roberson was in charge of five riders and a mess-wagon.

At our camp, west of Anton Chico, Pat Garrett met us, and we agreed to loan him a few of our "warriors." The writer turned over to him three men, Jim East, Lon Chambers and Lee Hall. Bob Roberson turned over to him three cowboys, Tom Emmory, Bob Williams, and Louis Bozeman.

We then continued our journey to White Oaks in a raging snow storm.

Pat Garrett started down the Pecos River with his crew, consisting of our six cowboys, his brother-in-law, Barney Mason, and Frank Stewart, who had been acting as detective for the Panhandle cattlemen's association.

At Fort Sumner, Pat Garrett deputized Charlie Rudolph and a few Mexican friends, to join the crowd which now numbered about thirteen men.

Finding that the "Kid" and party had been in Fort Sumner, and made the old abandoned United States Hospital building, where lived Charlie Bowdre and his half-breed Mexican wife, their headquarters, Pat Garrett concluded to camp there. He figured that the outlaws would return and visit Mrs. Charlie Bowdre, whose husband was one of the outlaw band.

In order to get a true record of the capture of "Billy the Kid" and gang, the author wrote to James H. East, of Douglas, Arizona, for the facts. Jim East is the only known living participant in that tragic event. His reputation for honesty and truthfulness is above par wherever he is known. He served eight years as sheriff of Oldham County, Texas, at

Tascosa, and was city marshal for several years in Douglas, Arizona.

Herewith his letter to the writer is printed in full:

"Douglas, Arizona,
May 1st, 1920.

Dear Charlie:

Yours of the 29th received, and contents noted. I will try to answer your questions, but you know after a lapse of forty years, one's memory may slip a cog. First: We were quartered in the old Government Hospital building in Ft. Sumner, the night of the first fight. Lon Chambers was on guard. Our horses were in Pete Maxwell's stable. Sheriff Pat Garrett, Tom Emory, Bob Williams, and Barney Mason were playing poker on a blanket on the floor.

I had just laid down on my blanket in the corner, when Chambers ran in and told us that the 'Kid' and his gang were coming. It was about eleven o'clock at night. We all grabbed our guns and stepped out in the yard.

Just then the 'Kid's' men came around the corner of the old hospital building, in front of the room occupied by Charlie Bowdre's woman" and her mother. Tom O'Folliard was riding in the lead. Garrett yelled out: 'Throw up your hands!" But O'Folliard jerked his pistol. Then the shooting commenced. It being dark, the shooting was at random.

Tom O'Folliard was shot through the body, near the heart, and lost control of his horse. 'Kid' and the rest of his men whirled their horses and ran up the road.

O'Folliard's horse came up near us, and Tom said: 'Don't shoot any more, I am dying.' We helped him off his horse and took him in, and laid him down on my blanket. Pat and the other boys then went back to playing poker.

I got Tom some water. He then cussed Garrett and died, in about thirty minutes after being shot.

The horse that Dave Rudabaugh was riding was shot, but not killed instantly. We found the dead horse the next day on the trail, about one mile or so east of Ft. Sumner.

After Dave's horse fell down from loss of blood, he got up behind Billy Wilson, and they all went to Wilcox's ranch that night.

The next morning a big snow storm set in and put out their trail, so we laid over in Sumner and buried Tom O'Folliard.

The next night, after the fight, it cleared off and about midnight, Mr. Wilcox rode in and reported to us that the "Kid," Dave Rudabaugh, Billy Wilson, Tom Pickett, and Charlie Bowdre, had eaten supper at his ranch about dark, then pulled out for the little rock house at Stinking Spring. So we saddled up and started about one o'clock in the morning.

We got to the rock house just before daylight. Our horses were left with Frank Stewart and some of the other boys under guard, while Garrett took Lee Hall, Tom Emory and myself with him. We crawled up the arroyo to within about thirty feet of the door, where we lay down in the snow.

There was no window in this house, and only one door, which we would cover with our guns.

The "Kid" had taken his race mare into the house, but the other three horses were standing near the door, hitched by ropes to the vega poles.

Just as day began to show, Charlie Bowdre came out to feed his horse, I suppose, for he had a moral in one hand. Garrett told him to throw up his hands, but he grabbed at his six-shooter. Then Garrett and Lee Hall both shot him in the breast. Emory and I didn't shoot, for there was no use to waste ammunition then.

Charlie turned and went into the house, and we heard the 'Kid' say to him: 'Charlie, you are done for. Go out and see if you can't get one of the s—of—b's before you die."

Charlie then walked out with his hand on his pistol, but was unable to shoot. We didn't shoot, for we could see he was about dead. He stumbled and fell on Lee Hall. He started to speak, but the words died with him.

Now Garrett, Lee, Tom and I, fired several shots at the ropes which held the horses, and cut them loose—all but one horse which was half way in the door. Garrett shot him down, and that blocked the door, so the 'Kid' could not make a wolf dart on his mare.

We then held a medicine talk with the Kid, but of course couldn't see him. Garrett asked him to give up, Billy answered, "Go to h—1, you long-legged s— of a b—!"

Garrett then told Tom Emory and I to go around to the other side of the house, as we could hear them trying to pick out a port-hole. Then we took it, time about, guarding the house all that day. When nearly sundown, we saw a white handkerchief on a stick poked out of the chimney. Some of us crawled up the arroyo near enough to talk to 'Billy.' He said they had no show to get away, and wanted to surrender, if we would give our word not to fire into them, when they came out. We gave the promise, and they came out with their hands up, but that traitor, Barney Mason, raised his gun to shoot the 'Kid,' when Lee Hall and I covered Barney and told him to drop his gun, which he did.

Now we took the prisoners and the body of Charlie Bowdre to the Wilcox ranch, where we stayed until next day. Then to Ft. Sumner, where we delivered the body of Bowdre to his wife. Garrett asked Louis Bousman and I to take Bowdre in the house to his wife. As we started in with him, she struck me over the head with a branding iron, and I had to drop Charlie at her feet. The poor woman was crazy with grief. I always regretted the death of Charlie Bowdre, for he was a brave man, and true to his friends to the last.

Before we left Ft. Sumner with the prisoners for Santa Fe, the 'Kid' asked Garrett to let Tom Emory and I go along as guards, which, as you know, he did.

The 'Kid' made me a present of his Winchester rifle, but old Beaver Smith made such a roar about an account he said 'Billy' owed him, that at the request of 'Billy,' I gave old Beaver the gun. I wish now I had kept it.

On the road to Santa Fe, the 'Kid' told Garrett this: That those who live by the sword, die by the sword. Part of that prophecy has come true. Pat Garrett got his, but I am still alive.

I must close. You may use any quotations from my letters, for they are true. Good luck to you. Mrs. East joins me in best wishes. Sincerely yours,

JAS. H. EAST."

The author had previously written to Jim East about "Billy the Kid's" sweetheart, Miss Dulcinea del Toboso. Here is a quotation from his answer, of April 26th, 1920: *"Your recollection of Dulcinea del Toboso, about tallies with the way I remember her. She was rather stout, built like her mother, but not so dark.*

"After we captured 'Billy the Kid' at Arroyo Tivan, we took him, Dave Rudabaugh, Billy Wilson, and Tom Pickett— also the dead body of Charlie Bowdre— to Fort Sumner.

"After dinner Mrs. Toboso sent over an old Navajo woman to ask Pat Garrett to let 'Billy' come over to the house and see them before taking him to Santa Fe. So Garrett told Lee Hall and I to guard 'Billy' and Dave Rudabaugh over to Toboso's, Dave and Billy being shackled together. As we went over the lock on Dave's leg came loose, and Billy being very superstitious, said: "That is a bad sign. I will die, and Dave will go free," which, as you know, proved true."

"When we went in the house only Mrs. Toboso, Dulcinea, and the old Navajo woman were there.

"Mrs. Toboso asked Hall and I to let 'Billy' and Dulcinea go into another room and talk awhile, but we did not do so, for it was only a stall of 'Billy's' to make a run for liberty, and the old lady and the girl were willing to further the scheme. The lovers embraced, and she gave 'Billy' one of those soul kisses the novelists tell us about, till it being time to hit the trail for Vegas, we had to pull them apart, much against our wishes, for you know all the world loves a lover."

It was December 23rd, 1880, when the "Kid" and gang, Dave Rudabaugh, Tom Pickett and Billy Wilson—were captured, and Charlie Bowdre killed.

The prisoners were taken to the nearest railroad, at Las Vegas, where a mob tried to take them away from the posse, to string them up.

They were placed in the County jail at Santa Fe, the capital of the Territory Of New Mexico, as the penitentiary was not yet completed.

Dave Rudabaugh was tried and sentenced to death for the killing of the jailer in Las Vegas. Later he made his escape and has never been heard of since.

CHAPTER IX.

"BILLY THE KID" IS SENTENCED TO HANG. HE KILLS HIS TWO GUARDS AND MAKES GOOD HIS ESCAPE.

In the latter part of February, 1881, "Billy the Kid" was taken to Mesilla to be tried for the murder of Roberts at Blazer's saw mill. Judge Bristol presided over the District Court, and assigned Ira E. Leonard to defend the "Kid." He was acquitted for the murder of Roberts.

In the same term of court, the "Kid" was put on trial for the murder of Sheriff Wm. Brady, in April, 1878. This time he was convicted, and sentenced to hang on the 13th day of May, 1881, in the Court House yard in Lincoln.

Deputy United States Marshall, Robert Ollinger, and Deputy Sheriff David Wood, drove the "Kid" in a covered back to Fort Stanton, and turned him over to Sheriff Pat Garrett.

As Lincoln had no suitable jail, an upstairs room in the large adobe Court House was selected as the "Kid's" last home on earth—as the officers supposed, but fate decided otherwise.

Bob Ollinger and J. W. Bell were selected to guard "Billy the Kid" until the time came for shutting off his wind with a rope.

The room selected for the "Kid's" home was large, and in the northeast corner of the building, upstairs. There were two windows in it, one on the east side and the other on the north, fronting the main street.

In order to get out of this room one had to pass through a hall into another room, where a back stairs led down to the rear yard.

In a room in the southwest corner of the building, the surplus firearms were kept, in a closet, or armory. One room was assigned as the Sheriff's private office.

The "Kid's" furniture consisted of a pair of steel handcuffs, steel shackles for his legs, a stool, and a cot.

Bob Ollinger, the chief guard, was a large, powerful middle-aged man, with a mean disposition. He and the "Kid" were bitter enemies on account of having killed warm friends of each other during the bloody Lincoln County war. It is said that Ollinger shot one of the "Kid's" friends to death while holding his right hand with his, Ollinger's, left hand. After this local war had ended, the fellow stepped up to Ollinger to shake hands and to bury the hatchet of former hatred. Ollinger extended his left hand, and grabbed the man's right, holding it fast until he had shot him to death. Of course this cowardly act left a scar on "Billy the Kid's" heart, which only death could heal.

J. W. Bell was a tall, slender man of middle age, with a large knife scar across one cheek. He had come from San Antonio, Texas. He held a grudge against the "Kid" for the killing of his friend, Jimmie Carlyle, otherwise there was no enmity between them.

In the latter part of April, Cowboy Charlie Wall had four Mexicans helping him irrigate an alfalfa field, above the Mexican village of Tularosa, on Tularosa River.

A large band of Tularosa Mexicans appeared on the scene one morning, to prevent young Wall from using water for his thirsty alfalfa.

When the smoke of battle cleared away, four Tularosa Mexicans lay dead on the ground and Charlie Wall had two bullet wounds in his body, though they were not dangerous wounds.

Now, to prevent being mobbed by the angry citizens of Tularosa, which was just over the line in Dona Ana County, Wall and his helpers made a run, on horseback, for Lincoln, to surrender to Sheriff Pat Garrett.

The Sheriff allowed them to wear their pistols and to sleep in the old jail. At meal times they accompanied either Bob Ollinger or J. W. Bell, to the Ellis Hotel across the main street, which ran east and west through town.

Charlie Wall did his loafing while recovering from his bullet wounds, in the room where the "Kid" was kept.

On the morning of April 28th, 1881, Sheriff Garrett prepared to leave for White Oaks, thirty-five miles north, to have a scaffold made to hang the "Kid" on. Before starting, he went into the room where the "Kid" sat on his stool, guarded by Ollinger, who was having a friendly chat with Charlie

Wall—the man who gave the writer the full details of the affair. J. W. Bell was also present in the room.

Garrett remarked to the two guards: "Say, boys, you must keep a close watch on the 'Kid,' as he has only a few more days to live, and might make a break for liberty."

Bob Ollinger answered: "Don't worry, Pat, we will watch him like a goat."

Now Ollinger stepped into the other room and got his double-barrel shot gun. With the gun in his hand, and looking towards the "Kid," he said: "There are eighteen buckshot in each barrel, and I reckon the man who gets them will feel it."

With a smile, "Billy the Kid" remarked: "You may be the one to get them yourself."

Now Ollinger put the gun back in the armory, locking the door, putting the key in his pocket. Then Garrett left for White Oaks.

About five o 'clock in the evening, Bob Ollinger took Charlie Wall and the other four armed prisoners to the Ellis Hotel, across the street, for supper. Bell was left to guard the "Kid."

According to the story "Billy the Kid" told Mrs. Charlie Bowdre, and other friends, after his escape, he had been starving himself so that he could slip his left hand out of the steel cuff. The guards thought he had lost his appetite from worry over his approaching death.

J. W. Bell sat on a chair, facing the "Kid," several paces away. He was reading a newspaper. The "Kid" slipped his left hand out of the cuff and made a spring for the guard, striking him over the head with the steel cuff. Bell threw up both hands to shield his head from another blow. Then the "Kid" jerked Bell's pistol out of its scabbard. Now Bell ran out of the door and received a bullet from his own pistol. The body of Bell tumbled down the back stairs, falling on the jailer, a German by the name of Geiss, who was sitting at the foot of the stairs.

JAMES W. BELL
DEPUTY SHERIFF
BORN—1853—DIED APRIL 28.1881
MURDERED BY WILLIAM BONNEY
A.K.A. "BILLY THE KID"
DURING HIS ESCAPE FROM THE
LINCOLN COUNTY JAIL
LINCOLN, N.M.

Of course Geiss stampeded. He flew out of the gate towards the Ellis Hotel.

On hearing the shot, Bob Ollinger and the five armed prisoners, got up from the supper table and ran to the street. Charlie Wall and the four Mexicans stopped on the sidewalk, while Ollinger continued to run towards the court house.

After killing Bell, the "Kid" broke in the door to the armory and secured Ollinger's shot-gun. Then he hobbled to the open window facing the hotel.

When in the middle of the street, Ollinger met the stampeded jailer, and as he passed, he said: "Bell has killed the "Kid." This caused Ollinger to quit running. He walked the balance of the way.

When directly under the window, the "Kid" stuck his head out, saying: "Hello, Bob!"

Ollinger looked up and saw his own shotgun pointed at him. He said, in a voice loud enough to be heard by Wall and the other prisoners across the street:" Yes, he has killed me, too!"

These words were hardly out of the guard's mouth when the "Kid" fired a charge of buckshot into his heart.

Now "Billy the Kid" hobbled back to the armory and buckled around his waist two belts of cartridges and two

Colt's pistols. Then taking a Winchester rifle in his hand, he hobbled back to the shot gun, which he picked up. He then went out on the small porch in front of the building. Reaching over the ballisters with the shotgun, he fired the other charge into Ollinger's body. Then breaking the shotgun in two, across the ballisters, he threw the pieces at the corpse, saying:" Take that, you s— of a b—, you will never follow me with that gun again."

Now the "Kid" hailed the jailer, old man Geiss, and told him to throw up a file, which he did. Then the chain holding his feet close together was filed in two.

When his legs were free, the "Kid" danced a jig on the little front porch, where many people, who had run out to the sidewalk across the street, on hearing the shots, were witnesses to this free show, which couldn't be beat for money.

Geiss was hailed again and told to saddle up Billy Burt's, the Deputy County Clerk's, black pony and bring him out on the street. This black pony had formerly belonged to the "Kid."

When the pony stood on the street, ready for the last act, the "Kid" went down the back stairs, stepping over the dead body of Bell, and started to mount. Being encumbered with the weight of two pistols, two belts full of ammunition, and the rifle, the "Kid" was thrown to the ground, when the pony began bucking, before he had got into the saddle.

Now the "Kid" faced the crowd across the street, holding the rifle ready for action.

Charlie Wall told the writer that he could have killed him with his pistol, but that he wanted to see him escape. Many other men in the crowd felt the same way, no doubt.

When the pony was brought back the "Kid" gave Geiss his rifle to hold, while he mounted. The rifle being handed back to him when he was securely seated in the saddle, then he dug the pony in the sides with his heels, and galloped west. At the edge of town he waved his hat over his head, yelling: "Three cheers for Billy the Kid!" Now the curtain went down, for the time being.

CHAPTER X.

"BILLY THE KID" GOES BACK TO HIS SWEETHEART IN FORT SUMNER, SHOT THROUGH THE HEART BY SHERIFF PAT GARRET AND BURIED BY THE SIDE OF HIS CHUM, TOM O'FOLLIARD.

A few days after the "Kid's" escape, Billy Burt's black pony returned to Lincoln dragging a rope. He had either escaped or been turned loose by the "Kid."

The next we hear of the "Kid" he visited friends in Las Tablas, and stole a horse from Andy Richardson. From there he headed for Fort Sumner to see his sweetheart, Miss Dulcinea del Toboso. It was said he tried to persuade her to run away with him, and go to old Mexico to live in happiness ever afterward. But that sweet little Dulce refused to leave mamma.

The "Kid" found shelter and concealment in the home of Mrs. Charlie Bowdre and her mother. One night a few weeks after his escape, the writer was within whispering distance of "Billy the Kid."

Myself and a crowd of cowboys had attended a Mexican dance. Mrs. Charlie Bowdre was there, dressed like a young princess. She captured the heart of the author, so that he danced with her often, and escorted her to the midnight supper.

About three o'clock in the morning the dance broke up and the writer escorted the pretty young widow, Mrs. Charlie Bowdre, to her adobe home. At the front door, I almost got down on my knees pleading for her to let me go into the house and talk awhile, but no use, she insisted that her mother would object.

Now a wine-soaked young cowboy with jingling spurs on his high-heel boots, staggered into camp and "piled" into bed, spread on the ground under a cottonwood tree, to dream of Mexican "Fandangos," where the girls have no choice of partners. Without an introduction the man walks up to the girl of his choice and leads her out on the floor to dance to his heart's content.

About six months later, in the fall of 1881, after the "Kid" had been killed, the writer was in Fort Sumner again, and attended a dance with Mrs. Charlie Bowdre. Now she explained the reason for not letting me enter the house. She said at that time, "Billy the Kid," who was in hiding at her home, was on the inside of the door listening to our conversation. That he recognized my voice.

Here Mrs. Bowdre told me the facts in the case, of how "Billy the Kid" met his death, bare-headed and bare-footed, with a butcher knife in his hand.

While in hiding in Fort Sumner the "Kid" stole a saddle horse from Mr. Montgomery Bell, who had ridden into town from his ranch fifty miles above, on the Rio Pecos.

Bell supposed the horse had been ridden off by a common Mexican thief. He hired Barney Mason and a Mr. Curington to go with him to hunt the animal. They started down the stream, Bell keeping on one side of the river, while Mason and Curington headed for a sheep camp in the foot hills.

Riding up to the tent in the sheep camp, the "Kid" stepped out with his Winchester rifle, and hailed them.

Barney Mason was armed to the teeth, and was on a swift horse. He had on a new pair of spurs and nearly wore them out making his get-away.

Mr. Curington rode up to his friend, "Billy the Kid," and had a friendly chat.

The "Kid" told Mr. Curington to tell Montgomery Bell that he would return his horse, or pay for him.

When Curington reported the matter to Mr. Bell, he was satisfied and searched no more for the animal.

After the "Kid's" escape from Lincoln, Sheriff Pat Garrett "laid low," and tried to find out the "Kid's" whereabouts through his friends and associates.

In March, 1881, a Deputy United States Marshal by the name of John W. Poe arrived in the booming mining camp of White Oaks. He had been sent to New Mexico by the Cattlemen's Association of the Texas Panhandle, Cattle King Charlie Goodnight, being the president of the association, had selected Mr. Poe as the proper man to put a stop to the stealing of Panhandle cattle by "Billy the Kid" and gang.

After the "Kid's" escape, Pat Garrett went to White Oaks and deputized John W. Poe to assist him in rounding up the "Kid."

From now on Mr. Poe made trips out in the mountains trying to locate the young outlaw. The "Kid's" best friends argued that he was "nobody's fool," and would not remain in the United States, when the Old Mexico border was so near. They didn't realize that little Cupid was shooting his tender young heart full of love-darts, straight from the heart of pretty little Miss Dulcinea del Toboso, of Fort Sumner.

Early in July, Pat Garrett received a letter from an acquaintance by the name of Brazil, in Fort Sumner, advising him that the "Kid" was hanging around there. Garrett at once wrote Brazil to meet him about dark on the night of July 13th at the mouth of the Taiban arroyo, below Fort Sumner.

Now the sheriff took his trusted deputy, John W. Poe, and rode to Roswell, on the Rio Pecos. There they were joined by one of Mr. Garret's fearless cowboy deputies, "Kip" McKinnie, who had been raised near Uvalde, Texas.

Together the three law officers rode up the river towards Fort Sumner, a distance of eighty miles. They arrived at the mouth of Taiban arroyo an hour after dark on July 13th, but Brazil was not there to meet them. The night was spent sleeping on their saddle blankets.

The next morning Garrett sent Mr. Poe, who was a stranger in the country, and for that reason would not be suspicious, into Fort Sumner, five miles north, to find out what he could on the sly, about the "Kid's" presence. From Fort Sumner he was to go to Sunny Side, six miles north, to interview a merchant by the name of Mr. Rudolph. Then when the moon was rising, to meet Garrett and McKinnie at La Punta de la Glorietta, about four miles north of Fort Sumner.

Failing to find out anything of importance about the "Kid," John W. Poe met his two companions at the appointed place, and they rode into Fort Sumner.

It was about eleven o'clock, and the moon was shining brightly, when the officers rode into an old orchard and concealed their horses. Now the three continued afoot to the home of Pete Maxwell, a wealthy stockman, who was a friend to both Garrett and the "Kid." He lived in a long, one-story adobe building, which had been the U. S. officers' quarters when the soldiers were stationed there. The house fronted south, and had a wide covered porch in front. The grassy front yard was surrounded by a picket fence.

As Pat Garrett had courted his wife and married her in this town, he knew every foot of the ground, even to Pete Maxwell's private bed room.

On reaching the picket gate, near the corner room, which Pete Maxwell always occupied, Garrett told his two deputies to wait there until after he had a talk with half-breed Pete Maxwell.

The night being hot, Pete Maxwell's door stood wide open, and Garrett walked in.

A short time previous, "Billy the Kid" had arrived from a sheep camp out in the hills. Back of the Maxwell home lived a Mexican servant, who was a warm friend to the "Kid." Here "Billy the Kid" always found late newspapers placed there by loving hands for his special benefit.

This old servant had gone to bed. The "Kid" lit a lamp then pulled off his coat and boots. Now he glanced over the papers to see if his name was mentioned. Finding nothing of interest in the newspapers, he asked the old servant to get up and cook him some supper, as he was very hungry.

Getting up, the servant told him there was no meat in the house. The "Kid" remarked that he would go and get some from Pete Maxwell.

Now he picked up a butcher knife from the table to cut the meat with, and started, bare-footed and bare-headed.

The "Kid" passed within a few feet of the end of the porch where sat John W. Poe and Kip McKinnie. The latter had raised up, when his spur rattled, which attracted the "Kid's" attention. At the same moment Mr. Poe stood up in the small open gateway leading from the street to the end of the porch. They supposed the man coming towards them, only partly dressed, was a servant, or possibly Pete Maxwell.

The "Kid" had pulled his pistol, and so had John Poe, who by that time was almost within arm's reach of the "Kid."

With pistol pointing at Poe, at the same time asking in Spanish, "Quien es?" (Who is that?), he backed into Pete Maxwell's room. He had repeated the above question several times.

On entering the room, "Billy the Kid" walked up to within a few feet of Pat Garrett, who was sitting on Maxwell's bed, and asked: "Who are they, Pete?"

Now discovering that a man sat on Pete's bed, the "Kid" with raised pistol pointing towards the bed, began backing across the room.

Pete Maxwell whispered to the sheriff: "That's him, Pat." By this time the "Kid" had backed to a streak of moonlight coming through the south window, asking: "Quien Es?" (Who's that?)

Garrett raised his pistol and fired. Then cocked the pistol again and it went off accidentally, putting a hole in the ceiling, or wall.

Now the sheriff sprang out of the door onto the porch, where stood his two deputies with drawn pistols.

Soon after, Pete Maxwell ran out, and came very near getting a ball from Poe's pistol. Garrett struck the pistol upward, saying: "Don't shoot Maxwell!"

A lighted candle was secured from the mother of Pete Maxwell, who occupied a nearby room, and the dead body of "Billy the Kid" was found stretched out on his back with a bullet wound in his breast, just above the heart. At the right hand lay a Colt's 41 caliber pistol, and at his left a butcher knife.

Now the native people began to collect,—many of them being warm friends of the "Kid's." Garrett allowed them to take the body across the street to a carpenter shop, where it was laid out on a bench. Then lighted candles were placed around the remains of what was once the bravest and coolest young outlaw who ever trod the face of the earth.

The next day, this, once mother's darling, was buried by the side of his chum, Tom O'Folliard, in the old military cemetery.

He was killed at midnight, July 14th, 1881, being just twenty-one years, seven months and twenty-one days of age, and had killed twenty-one men, not including Indians, which he said didn't count as human beings.

A few months after the killing of the "Kid," a man was coining money, showing "Billy the Kid's" trigger finger, preserved in alcohol. Seeing sensational accounts of it in the newspapers, Sheriff Garrett had the body dug up, but found his trigger-finger was still attached to the right hand.

During the following spring in the town of Lincoln, the sheriff auctioned off the "Kid's" saddle, and the blue barrel, rubber-handled, double action Colt's 41 caliber pistol, which the "Kid" held in his hand when killed.

There were only two bidders for the pistol, the writer and the deputy county clerk, Billy Burt, who got it for $13.50; Its actual value was about $12.00.

Since then many pistols have been prized as keepsakes from the supposed idea that the "Kid" had held each one of them in his hand when he fell. Many were presented to friends with a sincere thought that they were genuine.

As an illustration we will quote a few lines from a friendly letter, dated May 10th, 1920, written by the present game warden, Mr. J. L. DeHart of the state of Montana: "Later in March, 1895, I was ushered into office as sheriff of Sweet Grass County, Montana, and a former resident of New Mexico, and an acquaintance of 'Billy the Kid,' later a resident of Livingston, Montana, by the name of William Dawson, upon this momentous occasion, presented me with a splendid Colt's six-shooter, forty-five caliber, seven inch barrel, and ivory handle, said to have been the property of the notorious "Billy the Kid," when killed by Sheriff Pat Garrett, at the Maxwell ranch house. I have always considered this piece of artillery a valuable relic, and with much trouble have retained it. Most of my diligent watch, however, upon this gun, was brought about as a result of being named as state game warden in 1913, by His Excellency, Governor S. V. Stewart."

"Where ignorance is bliss, it is folly to be wise," is a true saying.

No doubt Mr. DeHart has felt proud over the ownership of the pistol "Billy the Kid" was supposed to have in his hand at the time of his death.

This is not the only "Billy the Kid" pistol in existence. It would be a safe gamble to bet that there are a wagon load of them scattered over the United States.

The Winchester rifle taken from the "Kid" at the time of his capture at Stinking Spring was raffled off in the spring of 1881, and the writer won it. He put it up again in a game of "freeze out" poker. As one of my cowboys, Tom Emory, was an expert poker player, I induced him to play my hand. I then went to bed. On going down to the Pioneer Saloon, in White Oaks, early next morning, the night barkeeper told me a secret, under promise that I keep it to myself. He said he was stretched out on the bar trying to take a nap. The poker game was going on near him. When he lay down all had been "freezed out" but Tom Emory and Johnny Hudgens. Just before daylight, Emory won all the chips, in a big show down, and I was the owner of "Billy the Kid's" rifle for the second time, but only for a moment, as Johnny Hudgens gave Tom Emory $20.00 for the gun, under the pretense that Hudgens had won it. Emory almost shed tears when he told me of losing the rifle in what he thought was a winning hand. Of course I didn't dispute it as I had given a promise to keep silent.

"Billy the Kid" came very near having a stone monument placed on his grave for the benefit of posterity—so that the curious among the unborn generations would know the exact spot where this "Claude Duval" of the southwest was planted.

One day, on the Plaza in the city of Santa Fe, in about the year 1916, the writer met Mrs. Gertrude Dills, wife of Lucius Dills, the Surveyor General of New Mexico, a daughter of Judge Frank Lea of White Oaks, and a niece to that whole-souled prince among men, the father of the city of Roswell, Captain J. C. Lea. She suggested that the writer get up a subscription to place a lasting monument on the grave of "Billy the Kid," so that future generations would know where he was buried. As a little girl, Mrs. Dills was once tempted to crawl under the bed, when "Billy the Kid" and gang shot up the town of White Oaks.

I at once went to the monument establishment of Mr. Louis Napoleon, and selected a fine marble monument, with the understanding that the inscription not be cut on it until after I had located the grave.

Many years ago, Will E. Griffin who is still a resident of Santa Fe, moved all the bodies of the soldiers buried in the old military cemetery, at Fort Sumner, to the National Cemetery at Santa Fe. He says when the work was finished, the only graves left in the grave-yard, were those of "Billy the Kid" and his chum, Tom O'Folliard. On these two graves, close together, still remained the badly rotted wooden head boards.

Since then the old cemetery has been turned into an alfalfa field, and the chances are, all signs of this noted young outlaw's resting place have been obliterated.

Soon after selecting the monument, I happened to be in the town of Tularosa, and brought up the subject to my old cowboy friend, John P. Meadows. He at once subscribed five dollars towards the erection of the monument. He said "Billy the Kid" had befriended him in 1879, when he needed a friend, and for that reason he would like to perpetuate his memory. He thought it would be no trouble to raise the desired amount in Tularosa, but the first man he struck for a subscription, Mr. Charlie Miller, former state engineer, discouraged him. Mr. Miller went straight up in the air with indignation at the idea of placing a monument at the grave of a bloodthirsty outlaw. Soon after this, Mr. Miller was murdered, when Poncho Villa made his bloody raid on Columbus, New Mexico.

This is as far as the grave of "Billy the Kid" came to being marked, as the writer has been too busy on other matters, to visit Fort Sumner and try to locate his last resting place.

In closing, I wish to state that with all his faults, "Billy the Kid" had many noble traits. In White Oaks, during the winter of 1881, the writer talked with a man who actually shed tears in telling of how he lay almost at the point of death, with smallpox, in an old abandoned shack in Fort Sumner, when the "Kid" found him. A good supply of money was given by the "Kid," and a wagon and team hired to haul him to Las Vegas, where medical attention could be secured.

Since the killing of the "Kid," Kip McKinney has died with his boots off, while Pat Garrett died with them on, being shot and killed on the road between Tularosa and Las Cruces, New Mexico. Hence the only man now living, who saw the curtain go down on the last act of "Billy the Kid's" eventful life, is John W. Poe, at the present writing is a wealthy banker in the beautiful little city of Roswell, New Mexico. He has served one term as sheriff of Lincoln County, and has helped to change that blood-spattered county from an outlaw's paradise, to a land of happy, peaceful homes.

Peace to William H. Bonney's ashes is the author's prayer.

THE END

We hope you enjoyed this book. For more great stories from our past, please visit the Historical Collection at our website.

Badgley Publishing Company

WWW.BadgleyPublishingCompany.com